AMAZING ORIGAMI

PLANT-EATING DINOSAURS

Gareth Stevens
PUBLISHING

Joe Fullman

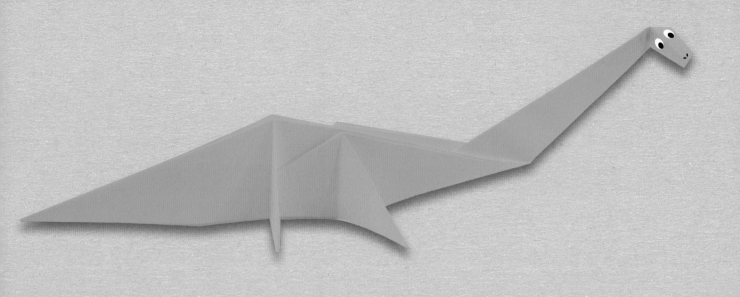

Please visit our website, **www.garethstevens.com**.
For a free color catalog of all our high-quality books,
call toll free 1-800-542-2595 or fax 1-877-542-2596.

Cataloging-in-Publication Data
Names: Pullman, Joe.
Title: Plant-eating dinosaurs / Joe Pullman.
Description: New York : Gareth Stevens Publishing, 2019. | Series: Amazing origami | Includes glossary and index.
Identifiers: ISBN 9781538234648 (pbk.) | ISBN 9781538234662 (library bound) | ISBN 9781538234655 (6pack)
Subjects: LCSH: Origami--Juvenile literature. | Dinosaurs in art--Juvenile literature.
Classification: LCC TT872.5 F85 2019 | DDC 736'.982--dc23

First Edition

Published in 2019 by
Gareth Stevens Publishing
111 East 14th Street, Suite 349
New York, NY 10003

Models created by Picnic
Photography by Michael Wilkes
Text by Joe Fullman
Design by Emma Randall

Printed in the United States of America

CPSIA compliance information: Batch #CW19GS: For further information contact Gareth Stevens, New York, New York at 1-800-542-2595.

CONTENTS

INTRODUCTION

Get ready for some fearsome folding as we explore the world of dinosaur origami. You'll learn how to make amazing plant-eating dinosaurs, from an almighty Apatosaurus to a spiky Stegosaurus.

A lot of the origami models in this book are made with the same folds and basic designs, known as "bases." This introduction explains some of the ones that will appear most, so it's a good idea to master these folds and bases before you start. When making the projects, follow the key below to find out what the lines and arrows mean.

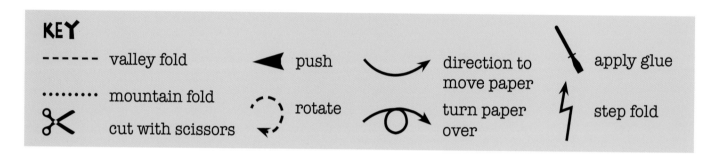

KEY
- - - - - - valley fold
·········· mountain fold
✄ cut with scissors
◀ push
◌ rotate
⌢→ direction to move paper
⟲→ turn paper over
✎ apply glue
⚡ step fold

VALLEY FOLD

To make a valley fold, fold the paper toward you, so that the crease is pointing away from you, like a valley.

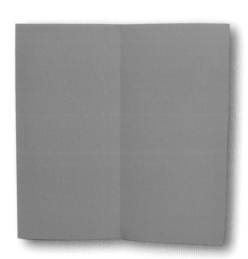

MOUNTAIN FOLD

To make a mountain fold, fold the paper so that the crease is pointing up toward you, like a mountain.

STEP FOLD

A step fold is used to make a zigzag in the paper. We'll use it to make ears, tails, and other dino features.

1 Valley fold the paper in half. Then make a mountain fold directly above the valley fold.

2 Push the mountain fold down over the valley fold and press down flat.

3 You now have a step fold. You can also make it in reverse, with the mountain fold first.

This is a useful fold if you want to flatten part of an origami model. It's a good way to create tails and snouts for your dinosaurs.

 1 Fold a piece of paper diagonally in half. Make a valley fold on one corner and crease.

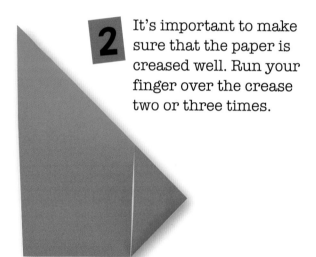

2 It's important to make sure that the paper is creased well. Run your finger over the crease two or three times.

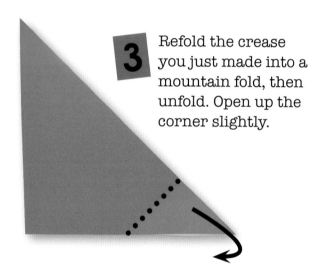

3 Refold the crease you just made into a mountain fold, then unfold. Open up the corner slightly.

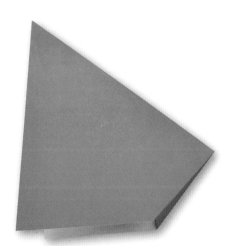

4 Open up the paper a little more and then tuck the tip of the corner inside. Close the paper. This is the view from the underside of the paper.

5 Flatten the paper. You now have an inside reverse fold.

OUTSIDE REVERSE FOLD

This is great if you want to make part of your model stick out. It will come in handy for making heads and crests.

 1 Fold a piece of paper diagonally in half. Make a valley fold on one corner and crease.

 **2** It's important to make sure that the paper is creased well. Run your finger over the crease two or three times.

3 Refold the crease you just made into a mountain fold, then unfold. Open up the corner slightly.

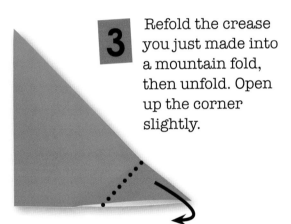

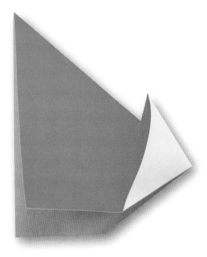

4 Open up the paper a little more and start to turn the corner inside out. Then close the paper when the fold begins to turn.

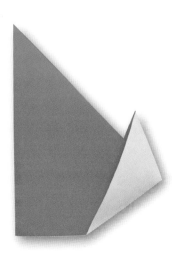

5 You now have an outside reverse fold. You can either flatten the paper or leave it rounded out.

KITE BASE

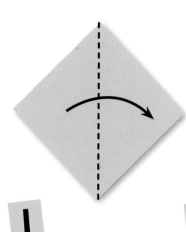

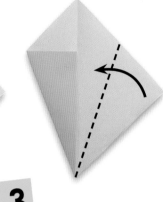

1 Place your paper like this. Valley fold it in half from left to right.

2 Valley fold the left-hand point over to the middle crease.

3 Repeat step 2 on the other side.

4 You now have a kite base.

WATERBOMB BASE

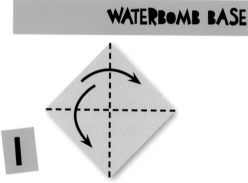

TURN OVER

45°

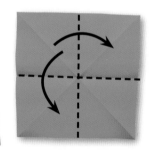

1 Make a fold from top to bottom and unfold. Then make a fold from left to right and unfold.

2 Turn your paper over and rotate it so that one side is facing you.

3 Fold from top to bottom and unfold. Then fold from left to right and unfold.

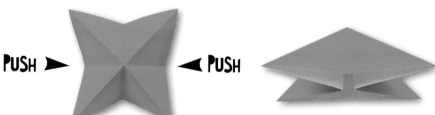

PUSH ▶ ◀ **PUSH**

4 Push the paper into this shape, so the middle point pops up.

5 Push the sides in, bringing the back and front sections together.

6 Flatten the paper. You now have a waterbomb base.

APATOSAURUS

Say "a-PAT-oh-SAW-rus"

From nose to tail, Apatosaurus was as long as a tennis court, making it one of the largest animals ever to walk the Earth. Your origami version will be a little smaller.

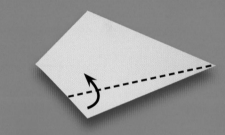

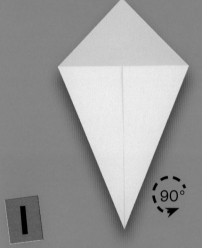

1
Make a kite base (see page 8), but start with the white side facing down, so your paper looks like this. Rotate it 90° to the left.

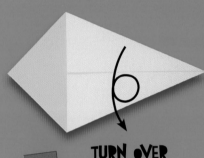

TURN OVER

2
Turn the paper over from top to bottom.

3
Fold the bottom point up to the central crease.

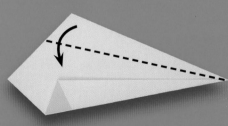

4
Fold the top point down to the central crease.

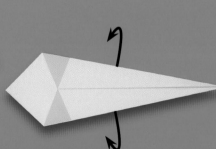

5
Unfold the lowest layer on both sides so that your paper matches the image in step 6.

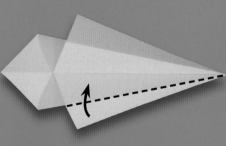

6
Fold the bottom point up to the middle along the crease line, turning it from a mountain fold to a valley fold.

9

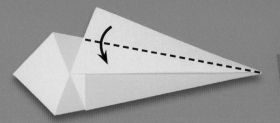

 7 Repeat step 6 with the top point.

8 On the lower half, lift the point of the top flap and bring it over to the right so it begins to form a triangle shape, as in the image in step 9.

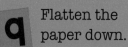 FLATTEN

9 Flatten the paper down.

10 Your paper should look like this. Repeat steps 8 and 9 on the top half.

11 Fold the bottom left point up to the central crease.

12 Repeat step 11 at the top of the paper.

 •PEN

13 Open up the fold you made in step 11 and start bringing the lower point over to the right, as in image 14.

FLATTEN

14 Flatten the point down so it forms a triangle shape.

15 Repeat steps 13 and 14 at the top.

16 Your paper should look like this. Mountain fold it in half from bottom to top.

 •PEN

17 Pull out the points to form the feet. Do the same on the other side.

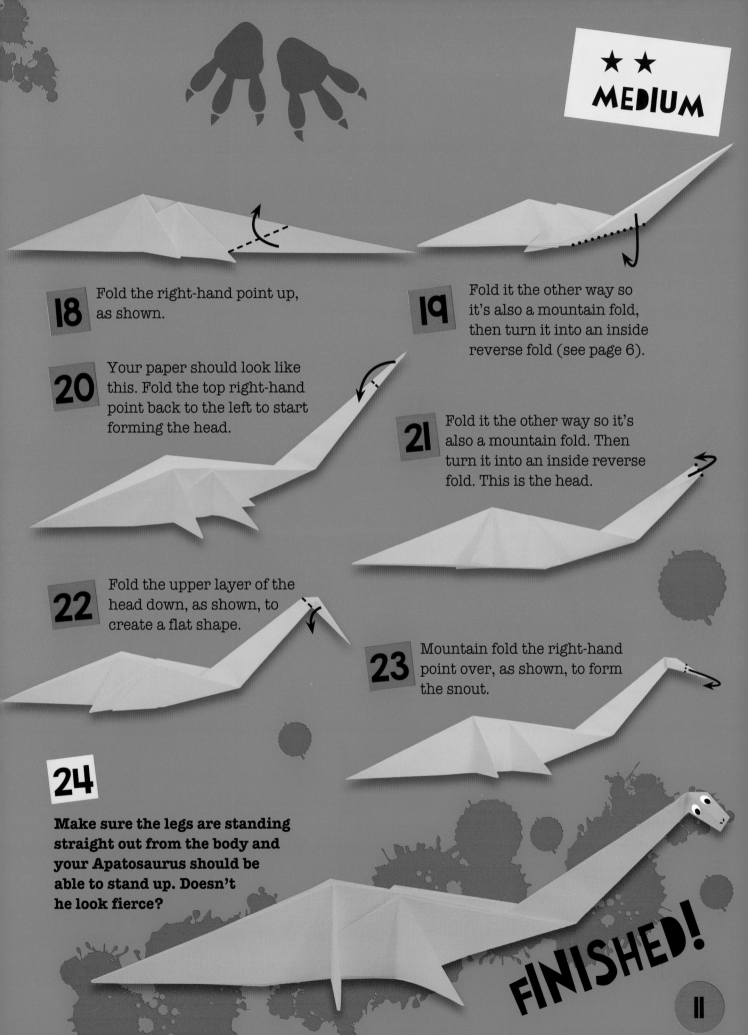

18 Fold the right-hand point up, as shown.

19 Fold it the other way so it's also a mountain fold, then turn it into an inside reverse fold (see page 6).

20 Your paper should look like this. Fold the top right-hand point back to the left to start forming the head.

21 Fold it the other way so it's also a mountain fold. Then turn it into an inside reverse fold. This is the head.

22 Fold the upper layer of the head down, as shown, to create a flat shape.

23 Mountain fold the right-hand point over, as shown, to form the snout.

24

Make sure the legs are standing straight out from the body and your Apatosaurus should be able to stand up. Doesn't he look fierce?

FINISHED!

IGUANODON

Say "ig-WAH-noh-don"

The Iguanodon had giant spiky thumbs it could use to fight off predators. This origami dino will require two pieces of paper: one for the body and one for the legs.

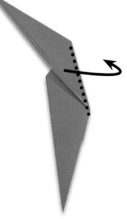

BODY

START WITH A KITE BASE

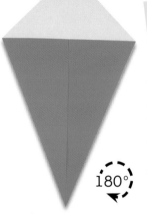

1 Take your first piece of paper and make a kite base (see page 8). Then rotate your paper 180°.

180°

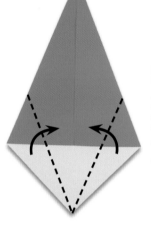

2 Fold the bottom left- and right-hand corners in to meet the central crease.

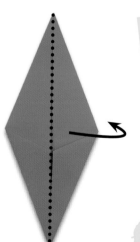

3 Mountain fold the paper in half along the central crease, from right to left.

4 Valley fold the top point over to the left, as shown.

5 Crease well and then fold back to the right, so it's also a mountain fold. Then turn it into an inside reverse fold (see page 6).

6

Your paper should look like this. Valley fold the top point back on itself, as shown. Crease well.

UNFOLD

7

Unfold the crease you made in step 6.

UNFOLD

8

Valley fold the top tip back again—this time folding it to the right.

q

Unfold the fold you made in step 8.

PUSH

10

Now push the central crease down over the two folds you made in steps 6 to 8 to create a step fold (see page 5). This is the head.

11

Your paper should now look like this. Fold the end of the head over, as shown.

TUCK

12

Tuck the fold into the head.

13

Your Iguanodon's body is ready. Put it to one side while you make the legs.

LEGS

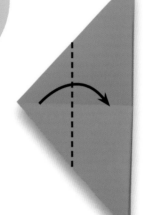

START WITH A WATERBOMB BASE

90°

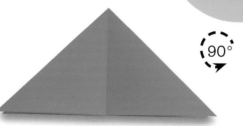

I Take the other piece of paper and make a waterbomb base (see page 8). Rotate it 90° to the left, so the tip of the triangle is facing left.

2 Valley fold the left-hand point to the right-hand edge of the paper.

3 Unfold the fold you made in step 2.

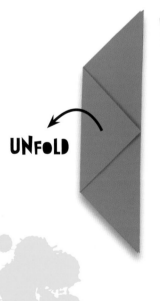

UNFOLD

4 Take hold of the upper layer of paper on the right-hand side and lift it over to the left, creating two pocket shapes.

LIFT

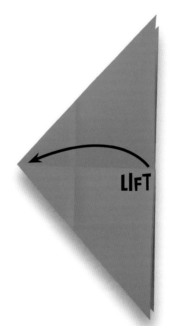

FLATTEN

FLATTEN

5 Your paper should look like this. Flatten it down at the top and bottom to create two white triangle shapes.

6

Fold the left-hand side (including the green triangle at the back) to the middle line, so the left-hand edge meets the central crease.

7

Make four valley folds, as shown. These are the feet. Now rotate your paper 180°.

180°

8

Dab some glue in the shaded areas. Then get the iguanodon body.

q

Place the body in the middle of the legs. Fold the legs down over the body.

10

Press the paper down hard, so that the legs stick to the body. Phew! After all that folding, your Iguanodon is ready to munch some leaves for lunch!

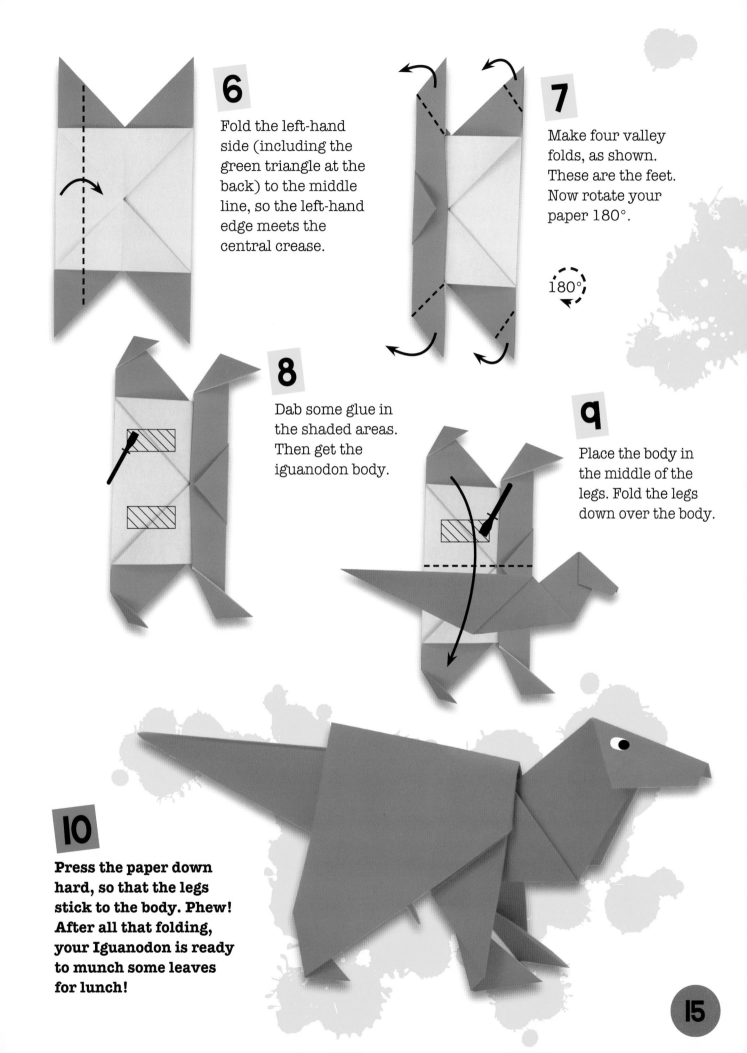

BRACHIOSAURUS

Say "BRACK-ee-oh-SAW-rus"

A bit like an enormous giraffe, this dino was one of the tallest creatures that has ever lived. You'll need a pair of scissors to complete this project.

START WITH A KITE BASE

1 Start by making a kite base (see page 8), then fold the paper in half from left to right.

2 Rotate the paper to the right so that it matches the image in step 3.

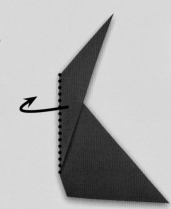

3 Fold the top point over to the right, as shown.

4 Fold it the other way, so it's also a mountain fold, then turn it into an outside reverse fold (see page 7).

FLATTEN

5 Your paper should look like this. Flatten it down.

6 Fold the top point over to the left, as shown.

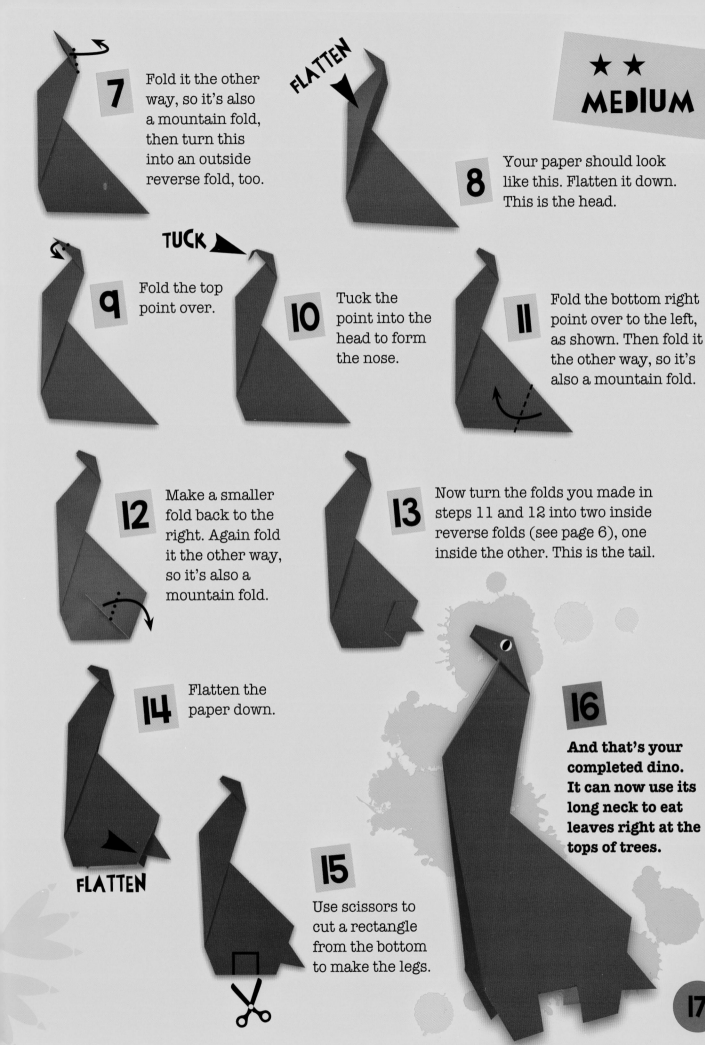

7 Fold it the other way, so it's also a mountain fold, then turn this into an outside reverse fold, too.

FLATTEN

8 Your paper should look like this. Flatten it down. This is the head.

★ ★
MEDIUM

TUCK

9 Fold the top point over.

10 Tuck the point into the head to form the nose.

11 Fold the bottom right point over to the left, as shown. Then fold it the other way, so it's also a mountain fold.

12 Make a smaller fold back to the right. Again fold it the other way, so it's also a mountain fold.

13 Now turn the folds you made in steps 11 and 12 into two inside reverse folds (see page 6), one inside the other. This is the tail.

14 Flatten the paper down.

FLATTEN

15 Use scissors to cut a rectangle from the bottom to make the legs.

16 And that's your completed dino. It can now use its long neck to eat leaves right at the tops of trees.

TRICERATOPS

Say "try-SER-ah-tops"

One of most famous dinosaurs, Triceratops is easy to recognize because of the three sharp horns on its head (its name means "Three-Horned Face"). You'll be making this dinosaur in two parts, starting with the tail.

TAIL AND BACK LEGS

1

Place your paper like this, white side up with a straight edge facing you. Valley fold in half from top to bottom, and unfold. Then valley fold in half from left to right, and unfold.

2

Fold the bottom edge up to the central crease.

3

Fold the left edge over to the central crease.

4

Fold the right edge over to the central crease.

5

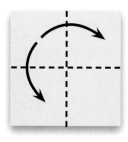

Fold the top left-hand corner over and down to the central crease.

6

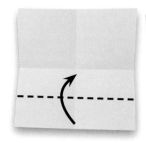

Fold the top right-hand corner over to the central crease.

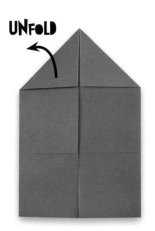

7

Open up the fold you made in step 5.

8

Bring the top central point of the fold down to form a pocket. Then flatten it down to form a triangle shape.

q

Your paper should look like this. Repeat steps 7 and 8 on the right-hand side.

10

Fold the top point down, as shown.

UNFOLD

11 Unfold the fold you made in step 10.

12 Fold the top point over to the right so it meets the crease you made in step 10.

UNFOLD

13 Unfold the fold you made in step 12.

14

Now fold the top point over to the left. Again, make sure it touches the crease you made in step 10.

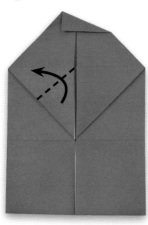

15

Fold the left-hand central point up and to the left.

16

Repeat step 15 on the right-hand side.

17

Make a fold on the left-hand side, as shown.

18

Repeat step 17 on the right-hand side.

UNFOLD

19

Unfold the fold you made in step 17.

20

Bring the left-hand point of the upper layer over to the right.

PUSH

FLATTEN

21

As you bring the point across, push the paper in as shown to make a new fold and then flatten the paper down.

22

Your paper should look like this. Repeat steps 19 to 21 on the right-hand side.

OPEN

23

Open up the paper on the bottom left-hand side.

24

Lift the central point up and over to the left, so that the paper forms a triangle shape.

25

Flatten the paper down.

FLATTEN

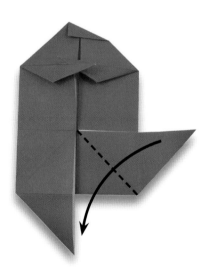

26

Your paper should look like this. Repeat steps 23 to 25 on the right-hand side.

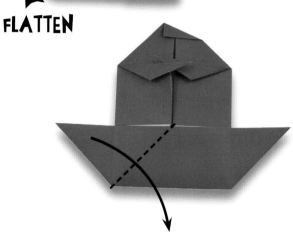

Fold the left-hand point down and to the right.

27

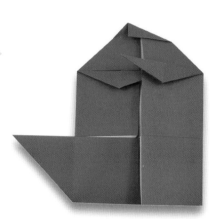

28

Fold the right-hand point down and to the left.

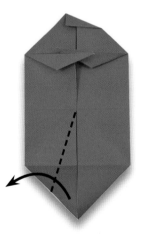

29

Fold the bottom left-hand point up and to the left, as shown.

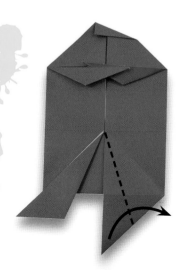

30

Fold the bottom right-hand point up and to the right.

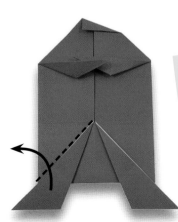

31

Fold the flap you made in step 29 over along its left edge.

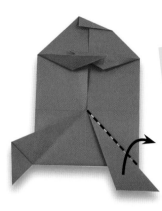

32

Now fold the flap you made in step 30 over along its right edge.

TURN OVER

33

Your paper should look like this. Turn it over from left to right.

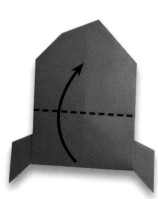

34

Fold the bottom edge of the paper up, as shown.

TURN OVER

35

Turn your paper back over from right to left.

36

Your legs are complete. Put them to the side while you continue with the head and front legs.

HEAD AND FRONT LEGS

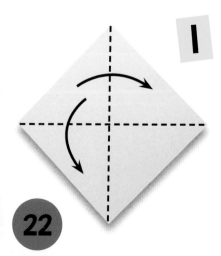

1

Take the second piece of paper and position it like this, white side up with a corner facing you. Fold it in half from top to bottom, and unfold. Then valley fold it in half from left to right, and unfold.

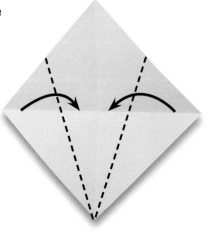

2

Fold the left-hand point and the right-hand point to the central line.

UNFOLD   **UNFOLD**

3

Unfold both sides.

4

Fold the top left edge over to the middle point, and unfold. Then fold the top right edge to the central point and unfold.

PUSH

PUSH

5

Fold the part of the central vertical crease marked with a dotted line the other way, so it's also a mountain fold. As you do, push in the sides and the top.

◄ PUSH

7

Your paper should look like this. Rotate it slightly to the left so it matches the image in step 8.

FLATTEN

6

As you push, the paper should begin to fold in on itself like this. Turn it to the left and flatten it down.

FLATTEN

FLATTEN

9

As you lift, the paper should form a pocket shape, like this. Flatten it down.

8

Lift the right-hand point up and over to the left.

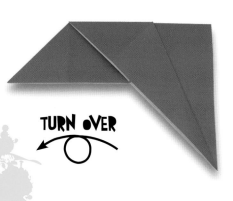

TURN OVER

10

Turn the paper over and repeat steps 8 and 9 on the other side. Then turn the paper back again so it matches step 11.

11

Fold the bottom right point so it lines up with the left-hand point.

UNFOLD

12
Unfold the fold you made in step 11.

13
Now fold the bottom right point up to the left at a slightly different angle, as shown.

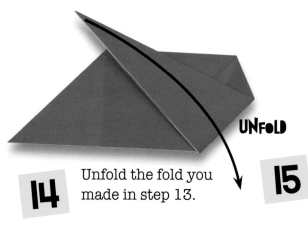

UNFOLD

14
Unfold the fold you made in step 13.

15
Push the right-hand point up and inside the paper along the fold lines you made in steps 11 and 13. As you do, fold the small triangles in the middle down and to the right.

PUSH

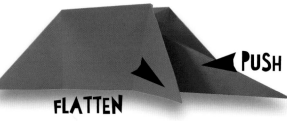

PUSH

FLATTEN

16
Keep pushing the right-hand point in, and flatten the triangle over the top.

OPEN

17
Open up the left-hand side so it forms a pocket.

24

FLATTEN ▶

18 Lift the middle point of the pocket up and to the right.

19 Flatten the paper down so it forms a square shape.

20 Make a fold on the right-hand side, as shown.

21 Turn your paper over and repeat step 20 on the other side. Then turn your paper back again.

TURN OVER

22 Now take the first piece of paper. Fold it in half and then unfold.

23 Dab some glue in the areas shown. Start to fold your paper in half again.

24 Place the first piece of paper over the second piece of paper and hold in place.

25 Once the glue has dried, you've got one terrifying Triceratops. Charge!

FINISHED!

STEGOSAURUS

Say "STEG-oh-SAW-rus"

This great big dino had a brain about the size of a walnut—so it probably wasn't very bright. Use two different types of paper to really make the plates on its back stand out.

HEAD AND BODY

1 Let's make the body and head first. Start with your paper like this, white side up with a flat edge facing you. Valley fold it in half from left to right, then unfold.

2 Fold the right-hand edge over to the central crease.

3 Fold the left-hand edge over to the central crease.

4 Fold the top-right point down to the central crease, as shown.

5 Repeat step 4 with the other three corners.

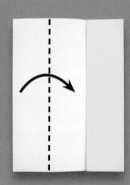

UNFOLD   UNFOLD

6 Unfold the folds you made in steps 4 and 5.

UNFOLD   UNFOLD

26

★ ★
MEDIUM

7 Open out the top right corner, and push the right edge down and to the left, so the crease folds the other way, as in the image for step 8.

8 Flatten the paper down.

9 Your paper should look like this. Repeat steps 7 and 8 with the other three corners.

10 Fold the top-right point of the upper layer down and to the left, as shown.

11 Fold the top left point down and to the right. It will go over the fold you made in step 10.

12 Repeat steps 10 and 11 with the bottom left and right points.

13 Your paper should look like this. Turn it over from left to right.

TURN OVER

14 Fold the top left-hand point over, as shown.

15 Fold the top right-hand point over.

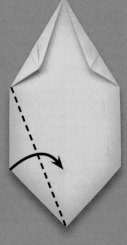

16 Fold the bottom left-hand point over to the central crease, as shown.

17 Fold the bottom right-hand point over to the central crease.

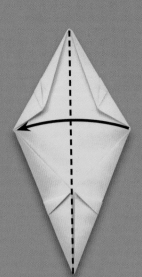

18

Your paper should look like this. Valley fold it in half from right to left.

19

Rotate the paper to the right.

90°

20

Mountain fold the left-hand point, as shown.

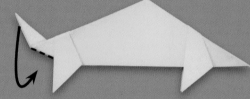

21

Fold it the other way, so it's also a valley fold, then turn it into an inside reverse fold (see page 6). This is the neck.

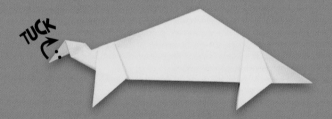

22

Make another mountain fold. Fold it the other way so it's also a valley fold, then turn it into an inside reverse fold. This is the head.

TUCK

23

Tuck the left-hand point up into the head to form the snout.

24

Your paper should look like this. Put it to one side while you make the plates with the other piece of paper.

PLATES

1

Place your paper white side up with a straight edge facing you. Valley fold it in half from top to bottom, and unfold. Then valley fold it in half from left to right, and unfold.

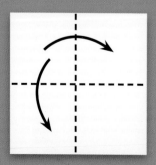

2

Fold the top right point down to the middle.

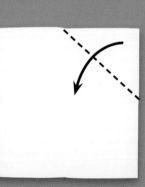

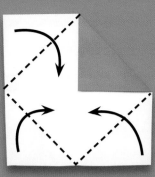

3 Repeat step 2 with the other three points.

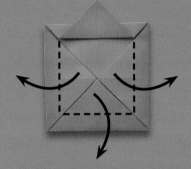

4 Fold the right-hand point into the middle.

5 Repeat step 4 with the other three points.

6 Fold the top point of the upper layer up, as shown.

7 Repeat step 6 with the other three points.

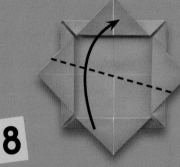

8 Fold the paper in half from bottom to top at a slight angle, as shown.

9 Your paper should look like this. Now grab the first piece of paper.

10 Slot the second piece of paper inside the first to complete your dino.

11 **Your spiky Stegosaurus is ready to take its first walk!**

FINISHED!

GLOSSARY

almighty Towering, huge, or extreme.

brain The organ animals use to sense and process information.

crease To fold.

enormous Extremely large.

fierce Violent or aggressive.

horn A hard, often pointed growth on an animal's skin.

plate A thin, flat structure on an animal's body, often made of hard material such as bone.

predator An animal that hunts and eats others for food.

rotate To turn.

terrifying When something causes extreme fear.

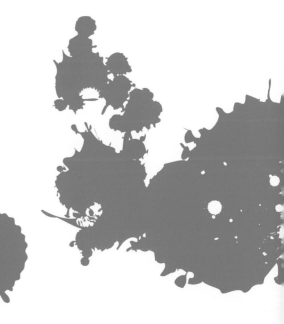
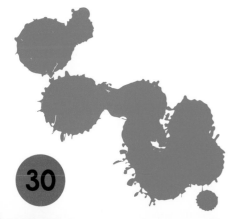

FURTHER INFORMATION

BOOKS

George, Anna. *Origami Dinosaurs: Easy & Fun Paper-Folding Projects.* Minneapolis, MN: Super Sandcastle, 2017.

Montroll, John. *Origami Dinosaurs for Beginners.* Mineola, NY: Dover Publications, 2013.

Ono, Mari, and Hiroaki Takai. *How to Make Paper Dinosaurs: 25 Awesome Creatures to Fold in an Instant.* London, UK: CICO Books, 2018.

Schultz, Walter-Alexandre. *Origami Dinosaurs.* New York, NY: Enslow Publishing, 2018.

WEBSITES

www.origami-make.org/howto-origami-dinosaur.php
Follow the instructions on this site to learn how to fold more dinosaurs.

www.origami-resource-center.com/origami-dinosaurs.html
This website offers instructions to make over 80 origami dinosaurs!

Publisher's note to educators and parents: Our editors have carefully reviewed these websites to ensure that they are suitable for students. Many websites change frequently, however, and we cannot guarantee that a site's future contents will continue to meet our high standards of quality and educational value. Be advised that students should be closely supervised whenever they access the Internet.

INDEX

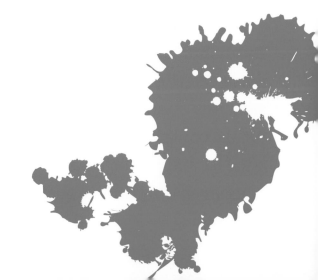